INSPIRATIONS

A collection of short poems

By

Keith Hearn

Copyright © Keith Hearn 2016

ISBN-13 978-1530345281
ISBN - 1530345286

1

Acknowledgements

I suppressed my love of writing for far too long. This was due partially to living in a different world to the one we live in today

Poetry is very personal

I hope that I can inspire others to write

Within the book I hope there is a poem for everyone

I have deliberately mixed up the poems

Enjoy

TWO ANGELS

An angel is a creature pure of soul
The symbol of an angel is such a powerful symbol
Angels provoke a dormant part of the mind
There is a mystical feel about a picture of an angel
They guard over us mortal beings, to ward off the
bad things in life

The angel is from a higher dimension
As I looked down at your leg I could see a tattoo of
an angel scored into your skin

An angel all of your own, so delicately drawn
I have two angels in my life for the price of one.

DREAM

Some people try so hard and dream of meeting the
right person
For me I feel that I have someone in the most
unlikely of places

There was no way in the world that I thought that
this would ever happen

You do not seem concerned about what other
people will say or think about our age difference
All I can think is how lucky I am

My thoughts are about how happy I will feel with
you in my life

I believe one day it will come true

SELFISH

Am I so selfish to want to be with someone as
beautiful as you?

I have tried so hard to put you off, the strategy does
not seem to have worked, you come back time and
time again

Each day you seem to grow on me, my feelings
grow stronger as time passes by

I would give up everything to make you happy

The Bill

Fighting over the bar bill

So many people talking and telling the confused
barman that they will pay the bill

All the barman wanted was to collect the payment,
he did not mind who was going to pay

That was easier said than done

All that could be heard were people raising their
voices offering to pay the bill, people saying that it
was their turn to pay the bill?

In the melee one little old lady paid the bill whilst
the rest were still discussing who was going to pay

As the barman gave the old lady her receipt both
smiled at the others

SHARING

Life is a wonderful thing, when sharing with a
loving person

LOVE

What is love, the word love is so powerful
Love can be a cheap and a throw away word
without any meaning

Frequently used by a throwaway society
It is a word that is sometimes used without any true
meaning

The word love, when used in the right
circumstances is such a powerful word

THE END OF DARK NIGHTS

For months the night and days have been so
depressingly dark and cold

The routine of going to sleep in the dark and waking
up to the dark on cold mornings

The days would drag, as the hours and minutes
slowly ticked away

All of a sudden the days become brighter and
warmer

In the mornings the light streams through the
curtains

It feels so nice to get out of bed in the mornings.
The morning light making the start of the day so
much more bearable

The heat of the sun warms up the morning

The flowers are beginning to pierce the soil like
spear tips

The world seems so much easier to face on a warm
sunny morning

WHO KNOWS

Who knows, indeed it is such a difficult question to answer It is one of life's loaded questions

One thing that I do know and it is something I cannot afford not to see what the future may bring me, and maybe then, who knows

If I stay and dispel any doubts and nerves, I might be pleasantly surprised and one day I could be the happiest person on the planet

FAITH

Am I being greedy for wanting so much more?

Life is too short that sometimes we have to take a
leap into the unknown

Where would we be if no one took that leap of
faith?

Join me and share the world together

All it takes is a leap of faith

REALITY

Sometimes people sit in their comfortable worlds,
letting life pass them by

Others fester and moan about life and do nothing to
change their ways

It take so much more to wake up and do something
with our lives

To take control of what is happening around us, to
steer our lives onto a truer course

I am sure people frown upon my life and what I am
doing with it, for the first time I feel free and in
control

MY WORLD

My world is not so exciting

I would give anything to be able to share my life
with another

I have to learn to lower the drawbridge and let that
someone enter my life

I dream of waking in the morning to have someone
beside me

Many years ago something deep inside of me was
killed off

To survive I have blocked all emotions and feelings

AGE

I look at you and wonder what you see in me
The age difference between us is so great it
sometimes feels like a huge chasm

To you the age difference means nothing, which is
the confidence of youth

Your youth is so intoxicating, I love the way you
are towards me

I on the other hand worry about the differences
I worry how people will react towards us

I would let you go so that you didn't get hurt

LONGING

I can see you whenever I want to and you never
complain or make a fuss

My eyes look at you from a distance
You stand there with so much pose and authority

Your eyes are so sharp and alive

How I long to be with you

To hold you close and to tell you how I feel for you

THE TAR BRUSH

How did I, the one who is older and allegedly more experienced, lose my head and heart to a beautiful lady?

My experiences of the fairer sex has left me suspicious and insecure, I cannot tar you with the same brush

I want to let my heart run free and to wallow in the feeling of love

Should I share in the happiness that this lady so freely offers?

Only time will tell

SMILE

You have the knack of making me smile
I love the way you reassure me regardless of my
attitude

I look at you and realise how lucky I am to have
you in my life

You are melting the ice surrounding my heart

You have taught me how to feel loved once again

GIVING

How I long to be loved and to give my love back by
the shovel full

I have so much love and kindness to give to
someone

I do believe that I scare the fairer sex away because
I may seem desperate and needy

I suppose it is because I have not had the love of
someone for many years

I am told that I am very nice and kind, as much as it
is nice to hear the words it is the love and closeness
of another that I miss

Maybe one day a special person will enter my life
and complete the circle of love and happiness once
again

TECHNOLOGY

As I sit listening to music and writing poetry with
you in mind, I worry that you will not like me in the
flesh

This is the modern way of making contact with
someone via social media

I check my mobile phone or laptop to see if I have a
message from you

It is all new to me as in the past the only way to
come into contact with someone was to meet them
face to face

I have grasped the modern medium with both hands
It is a different world for a woman meeting on blind
dates

Social media is open to all sorts of abuse and no one
can take risks
Am I placing too much onto your shoulders?

WITHIN

I realise that there is an age gap between us
Initially I thought that it was too much of a gap, I
soon realized that it is the person within that is most
important not the age of someone

Your messages are full of concern and care for me
I have grown so attached to you and I care so much
for you

I count myself so lucky to have you contacting me,
others may have their own view

We could be so good for one another, you inspire
me to write and write
I
I hope in return that I make you happy and to feel
wanted

We all need to feel wanted by someone

SOMEWHERE OUT THERE

We have never met and yet you have captured my
imagination
How I wish that I could be with you to tell you how
I feel for you
This is very surreal to me, my thoughts are why I
have feelings for someone that I have never met
We have never met across a room, nor have we had
the pleasure of our eyes meeting across a packed
room, our eyes locking together knowing that there
is something special
There is one thing that we do not have or shared is
to be together

PINK

Oh how I like your persona as "Pink" but you are
not the person that you think that you think you are

You are a beautiful lady
Yet another who has been hurt in the past

Who thinks that she wants to have fun as someone
else, but in fact just wants the closeness and love of
another?

I have "bumped" into you solely by chance maybe
it is fate who knows?

I know that you would turn heads if you were with
me

You are such a loving person

TAKE MY BREATH AWAY

Your beauty takes my breath away, your olive skin
tone, you have a well-defined bone structure

From a distance you hold your bearing with such
grace

You are so well spoken and well mannered, without
the airs and graces

I like the way that you take your time to say hello
and to chat even though you are so busy

I cannot remember the last time that someone took
my breath away as you do

THE SIGNS OF SUMMER

On a summers morning to lay in bed is such a
decadent feeling

With the sun breaking through the window,
crashing through the closed curtains

The sun's rays filling the room just like a
comforting blanket, the heat from the sun making
the start to the day feel so lazy and pleasant

Bird song filling the air with the wonderful sounds
of nature

Opening the curtains and the windows to the
cacophony of bird song

The scene makes one think that we can take on
anything that the world can dish up

THE OPEN FIRE

The heat from an open fire in winter is such a
comforting site

It becomes the focal point of a room

People make a bee line towards the fire it seems to
draw people towards it

It attracts everyone's gaze

Maybe I should transform into an open fire and be
the centre of attention

POSITIVITY

You are such a positive lady

Whenever I watch your videos or read your positive
notifications
You come across as an extremely positive person

You ooze positivity

I smile at your large bright eyes they emphasize
what you are trying to say

You believe in yourself and your enthusiasm is so
catching

Thank you for counting me as your friend

CHANCES

I have never told you my innermost thoughts
My wish is for both of us to have a future together
is that too much to ask for?

I do not want you to waste your life
What I am trying to say is that I have feelings for
you I only want you to have a life of your own
My life is about to take off once again and I have
had a second bite of the cherry

I often wonder if this chance to be happy again will
ever come around again in my life time

Thank you for giving me a second chance of life

RELATIONSHIP

Why do I seem to ruin everything that is good for
me?

I want everything to be just right, perfect, life is not
like that

The trouble is I have forgotten what a loving
relationship is all about

It feels like hunting for the Holy Grail
A relationship it is about two people

I have to learn to compromise and not to steam roll
my wants and needs onto someone else

FORGIVNESS

I find that you are a very forgiving person
Others would have left me by now, they would have
ran for the hills

I realise that I am such hard work, I just cannot help
being so passionate

Over the years I have built up such a protective
shell

Bit by bit you are chipping away at my outer layers
I am truly sorry that this has been a very difficult
journey for you

If you steal my heart I will be yours for ever

I find you so adorable and refreshing

ON THE DANCE FLOOR

We will never dance again

Never destined to dance the night away

Destiny can play such a cruel tricks, not knowing
what is around the next corner

To dance with you, all smiling and happy

The beat of the music playing away, while we are
together we are oblivious to all around

I tried so hard to make our last day last as long as
possible

EYES

Your eyes give you away

Angry, searching, happy and watch your step eyes

Eyes are the gateway to the soul

Your laughter eyes are your most expressive feature

You light up like a beacon in the darkness

I see the impish girl through your eyes

THE SUN

The sun beaming down and warming up the air on a
crisp spring day

It is the first sign of winter passing on by

Everyone feels so much better with the first signs of
spring

It is the first signs that winter has passed on by

So many people are outdoors cycling, walking and
running

It draws so many people out from their homes

The dreariness of winter is passing by

The first signs of sunny times feels so much better
than the drabness of the winter months

SCREAM

I see a complicated person someone who is
screaming out for love and attention

I can feel the hurt that you feel

All that I have ever wanted is to feel your love

We can have all the love in the world

It is there for the asking

WRITE

My life has been full of regrets and the need to re-write the pages of history

From my experiences I know that it is impossible to re-write history

The only thing that can be done is to write about the future so that the past does not have to drag one down into the abyss

To look forward and not to look back is the way to move forward it is the only way to be positive

TIME

Time passes by so fast

One day we are so young and we wish away the
hours, days, weeks and years

As we become older we think that there isn't
enough hours in the day

Everyone can remember wishing away our days

All we ever remember is where has the time gone

VIBRANCE

The winter weather is quickly passing by

The green of the landscape is appearing all around

The fields are becoming a deeper green

The seeds have germinated and their young shoots
are poking through the soil

Everything looks so new and vibrant

Spring is in the air
Nature is a making a splash of colour on the
landscape

PASTY

The lady from the deli makes me smile every time I
buy a pasty

She is such a pleasant person

Even though she laughs at my corny jokes and by
calling her by the wrong name

She grins and bears my juvenile humour

I am always served with a courteous grin and
service

Oh how she must dread me turning up for my pasty

EMOTIONS

What we have is what dreams are made of
I feel like I am in touching distance of having a
happy life

I have so much to give
It was you who said that I would have a sad life if I
withdrew from the world
Your words ring so true

You have helped me from running away and to face
up to my emotions and past

I don't think you have any idea of what you have
done to me

I know that you would enrich my world if you
joined me

I hope that I have helped you
Can we turn our dreams into reality?

WHO KNOWS

No one knows what the future may hold

One thing that is known, are my feelings for you
I know that I will cherish you for as long as you
want me to

My life will be fulfilled with someone in my life
I know that I would be so happy

Who knows what the future may hold

SHARE

I do wish that we could share the everyday things
that others take for granted

My life is moving on and hopefully towards
something better, no more hurt no more looking
over my shoulder

I would like to invite you to share in the good times
I realize that you have much to give up

To share in one another's lives will be just the start
of the rest of our lives

REALITY

My head tells me that this will not work, my heart
tells me that it will because my heart is scarred by
so much hurt over the many years

My head wants the love and the comfort that love
brings

My head tells me that what we have is not real

My heart wants it to be real and for it to work

MY BEAUTY

How beautiful you look in your picture
You look so confident and happy

Your pose is so striking

Your pretty eyes are looking directly towards me
How perfect you look

YOU AND I

Your fresh eyes immediately caught my attention

Your makeup highlights the whites of your pretty eyes

I could not help but notice your eyes staring back at me

I want to be close to you to you pull you close me to tell you that we will be travelling on a magical journey together

CLOSENESS

For so many years I have enjoyed my own company
I never thought that I needed someone in my life
I did not believe that another person would wish to
know me

I had shut myself off from others around me
Then one day I realized that I do miss the closeness
of another

At first I would rush into relationships but I was
soon to find that life and relationships are not
formed this way

Relationships take a long time to mature and to be
true

I still find myself on my own, this is not from the
lack of trying

UNFREQUENTED

Unfrequented feelings, in all my years I have never been treated with as much hatred as you have bestowed upon me

I only had to see you and you would melt my heart

You made it perfectly clear that you are not interested in me

It hurt just like a knife being plunged into my heart the pain is so deep

Whenever I saw you the same feelings ran deep

I don't hate you but I know that you hate me with such passion and relish

Will the pain ever end?

SURPRISES

Life is full of surprises, nobody knows what is
around the next corner

In the past my life had structure I knew what would
happen from one day to the next

Now life throws up so much, there are times that
life is not such a bad thing as nothing shocks me
anymore

No one knows what fate is or what it means, it isn't
something that is planned it just happens it appears
from no where

Being spontaneous is a good thing, there are people
who do not like surprises

Life is the biggest surprise

A BEAM OF LIGHT

A beam of bright light has descended upon me

It has forced me to sit up and take notice

Feelings that have been dormant for many years
have been awoken

You wear an angel as a reflection of your inner self
You have touched me in a way that I shall never
forget

You are such an affectionate person
If I shall never meet you I would like you to know
that I will never forget you

PRINCESS

I can see you in the distance fluffing up your shiny jet black hair, which cascades around your elegant face, you look like an Arabian princess

Your deep dark brown eyes pierce the air as you look around the room

You are such a sensual person who is very caring, sincere and kind

I could tell immediately that you are a very ambitious and determined person

OPEN SECRETS

When you decided to open up to me

Many would have run to the hills or may have pre-judged you

To me you were someone wanting to open up and to tell me everything about yourself

For me what you told me I have to accept as it is who you are

I adore you it was such a risk that you took to tell me of your past

I have reflected on your candidness
Sometimes in life we can be too open and it can backfire

THE PLATFORM

It was such an eye opener observing people
queueing for the early morning train to London
People were queueing for either the stopping or the
cross country train

People stood in the same place on the platform
every day, some would silently stand behind a
stranger, and others formed a silent orderly queue
behind that person

When I first saw this ritual I thought that it was
such a strange practice Until an approaching train
pulled up to the platform it was at this point that I
realized that they were standing at the precise spot
to board the carriage

It is the cattle instinct that is within everyone

THE OLD SEA CAPTAIN

Many a time the sea captain would come into the
pub for a beer or two

He would regale to those at the bar telling all who
would listen to his old sea yarns about captaining
his tugs up and down the coast of Britain and
Ireland

Mentioning places as far afield as Ellesmere Port
and what it looked in the early morning light

Or how a tow rope on his tug had slipped allowing a
large barge to slip away from the tug into the dense
fog and knowing how dangerous the situation was.
How it took him hours to find the barge and to
secure it back onto the tug

As he reminisce, he smiles, possibly with the
memory, or the thought of those around him were

Engrossed in his yarns of the seas, as he takes
another sip of his beer

He must have so many stories of the sea and the
storms he had encountered on board his trusted tug
battling against the cruel seas

KAPITAN

The new crew that boarded the tug referred to the
Captain, as the "Kapitan"

He had the look of a German "U" boat Kapitan
One can imagine him looking through a submarine
periscope with his cap turned the opposite way

The Captain had a peppery beard like most sailors
He does not like being on "dry" land for too long.
Even though when he is at sea he moans and wishes
to be back on dry land

The sea is his calling

"DIN DINS"

I laughed when I heard the landlady of the village
pub say to a diner how is your "Din Dins"

I looked around thinking that she was talking to a
couple with children

I soon noticed that she was talking to an elderly
couple with no children in sight

I said to her "Din Dins what was that all about?"

She said "just friendly customer service" with a
smile on her face, I thought it was amusing and
laughed

She retorted "watch it or you are working here
tonight"

Oh how we laughed

PUB NOISES

As I was sat in the pub writing my poems

The pub has so much atmosphere, so many different
people from all walks of life, some eating some
having a drink

I wonder what stories they must have locked away

As time goes by there is more chatter, some people
raising their voices, some are laughing and some are
looking so sad

There are other people on their own, possibly
waiting for another?

The sound of glasses chinking and bottle tops being
eased off and poured into a glass. The sound of a
cork being eased off a bottle of champagne

Soft music being played in the background it all
adds to the atmosphere of the pub

SENSIBLE

You are the sensible one out of the pair of us
I worry so much about what you will think of me
when we meet

I am meant to be the sensible one. I am also the one
who wants things to happen immediately

You are the one who needs more time, to take
things slowly, you are the one with your feet firmly
on the ground

You are the one who will help change my life
I hope that I can help change your life for the better
We both realize that this could be life changing

INSPIRATION

You inspire me to write, when I am feeling down
and don't feel like writing anymore, as soon as I
receive a message from you I feel the urge to write

My thoughts are always about you, thinking about
what you are doing at the precise moment

I think about your journey into work and what you
are wearing and if you are feeling happy or sad?
I think about what you are saying to your friends
about your feelings towards me

You inspire me in so many ways

KNOCK KNOCK

I don't understand how love works

I never expected it to come knocking on my door
once more

At first I did not know what it was I did not
recognize the feeling

My life was trudging along one day would merge
into another, just a normal mundane life

Then all of a sudden out of the blue, you came
along a highly intelligent, beautiful woman who has
turned my life upside down

I have caused you a lot of hurt and pain I have no
excuses apart from I was fighting the fears and
emotions coursing through my mind

THE FUTURE

What can happen in the future it is such an
unknown quantity

If I could look into the future I would make a
fortune

I can only wish for the good things in life

Things that money cannot buy

That is my wish for the future

HOPE

Hope everyone has hope in their heart, the hope of a
rich and loving relationship

To grow with another and to learn and appreciate
one another

To nurse someone back to health when they are sick
and ill

Sometimes I dream too much

Maybe I live in another world, a much simpler
world, devoid of hurt and mistrust

Life is naturally full of ups and downs

Maybe the lady of my dreams will walk into my life
and set it alight

Who knows!!

HAPPINESS

During Christmas over the noise of the pub, party
goers can be heard enjoying the festivities

The sound of laughter and the raised voices and
people enjoying themselves

In the distance I can hear party poppers and the snap
of Christmas crackers

The sound of champagne corks

Everyone is in a festive mood People with their
partners out to enjoy one another's company

CLOSENESS

Only the love of a good woman, can make a man
feel calm

No matter what a man has gone through in life

A woman can get to the true heart of a man and
reduce him to tears

We all need the love of another person

It has been a long time since I have allowed another
person to get close to me

It is not such an easy thing to do

It takes a special person to pierce my heart once
again

THE HUMAN RACE

Humans are meant to be the most intelligent animal on the planet? The difference is that we kill one another on such an industrial scale

We are destroying the planet that we share with other species

Whenever we meet other people from different parts of the world, we may not speak the same language, we seem to be able to communicate and understand one another

We laugh at similar things and enjoy similar things there is an unspoken bond

Life is not too dissimilar, as Nations we seem to want to destroy one another

It has been the same since the beginning of time we
seem to fail on the quest to find peace between
Nations

It is time to act now before Mother Nature takes her
revenge on the Human Race

FUTURE

Who knows what the future may hold

People would make a fortune if we could predict the future

Who would want to know what the future may hold, it would be such a boring world indeed

I like the world as it is, with its surprises including the good and bad

If I could see into the future I might be sorely disappointed in what I could see

TAKEN FOR GRANTED

It is time that I found happiness something that
many people take for granted

In the past I have doubted people's intentions
towards me

So many times I have pushed loving people away

I have to learn that not everyone is out to hurt me

I have to accept other people's kindness and love
and to embrace who they are, and not what they are

TO LET YOU IN

I wonder if you will be able to peal the many layers
of protection I have built around my heart

Will you be the one who has the time and patience
to unlock my heart and be able to accept my love in
return?

It will take time for me to let you in But let you in I
will

Once you turn the key and unlock my heart, the
feeling will be just like fireworks exploding in the
sky

All you have to do is to remove the many layers
protecting my heart

I WONDER

I wonder how the lady in red is getting on

She stands on the platform waiting for the 07:01 am
train to Southampton

She sits down on the platform bench, looking so
prim and proper

On the train she reads an eBook or watches a film
on her electronic device, sat giggling to herself

Whilst travelling on the train she sits nibbling on
her freshly made sandwiches

Once the train pulled into her station she would rush
to catch a bus outside the station

She was a very pleasant lady, dressed in her red
coat, which made her stand out from the crowd

THE BROTHERS

"Oh are you drinking that cooking lager again"?

Each time a round of drinks is purchased the same
rallying cry rings out

The "brothers" think that they are a pair of
comedians they are the only two at the bar that
laugh at their own jokes

Everyone in the bar are chatting less the two
brothers who are texting on their mobile phones

After further rounds of drinks one of the brothers
would burst into song whilst the other brother is
prone to mimicking those who newly arrive at the
pub. He would copy their mannerisms which is
very funny and people have a good old laugh while
the other brother is still singing

The brother who is singing keeps piping up with "is your book ready yet?" This would prime the other

Brother to the fact that my novel had not been published

I would never hear the last of it

It made everyone in the bar laugh and gave them something to talk about, it was so funny

TRAPPED

As the woman got closer and closer, I could not
miss her, she had her child in her grasp

The woman was staring into a far off place, her eyes
so vacant just like black pits looking out onto a
world that she did not seem to fit into or belong

Her skeletal figure oh so thin, so stick like Her
clothes hanging from her skeletal frame It made me
think what nightmare is she living

A sound emitted from her mouth "spare some
change for a cup of tea mister". At the same time
she held out her skeletal hand

Her child remained silent, with a look of horror on
her face

Trying to earn some money for her next fix, perhaps
who knows?

Such a waste of a life

JOLLY

Oh what a jolly little girl you are. Always smiling,
always giggling

Such a lovely little girl, she has made my life a lot
more enjoyable

How lucky we are to have such a child touch our
lives

How wonderful it feels to be able to say I am your
grandfather

What a jolly little girl you are

THE WALK TO SCHOOL

Getting up in the mornings to go to school always
seemed so cold

As we walked down our street on the way to school,
dragging our heels, making the journey last as long
as possible

The smells and the breeze coming off the river
Mersey merged with the smells of coal burning
from the terraced housing and the smells of the
alleyways

The journey to school should only take five minutes
at the most

Someone always had a football we would entertain
ourselves on the long journey to school. Every day
we passed Ringo Starr's old house I would wonder
if he made the same journey to St Silas's school

INSPIRATIONS

It was such a short trip to school we made the most
of the journey

It seemed even shorter and quicker trip at the end of
school

THE DANCER

As soon as she flew into the room, she looked so tasty

She danced so gracefully, she looked as though she was dancing on air, she seemed to love the thrill of the dance. She buzzed from one table to the next

As I watched from deep within the shadows, I was waiting for her to tire

She danced towards me, she got closer and closer. The music and her dancing was so intoxicating

Into my silky web she flew. Too tired to struggle

I had waited so long for this moment

COLD

The cold creeps up my body, like the tide lapping up onto a beach, the cold creeps up my toes and into my feet

At the tips of my body, my fingers are becoming colder and colder, my hands turning blue

My nose is becoming bluer and darker, it is excruciatingly painful the tips of my ears are in such pain

My body is starting to shut down. I can feel the energy ebbing from my lifeless body

Each movement is becoming slow and painful

Sleeping under the stars is so lonely and cold

Overnight my body shuts down for good

RUSH

People scurrying from one place to another, rush, rush, rush

No one seems to want to talk to one another, only to keep on rushing from here and there

If only people would slow down and take the time to talk to one another, this does not seem to be on anyone's mind apart from rush, rush, rush

Something suddenly happens that makes everyone stop, someone has fallen over in the street, people stop to help, all of a sudden no one is rushing anymore, and people are talking once again

The person who fell eventually gets up and carries on with their journey

Once again everyone is scurrying from one place to another rush, rush rush

RELAX

Sat at the bar relaxing observing other's working,
whilst enjoying myself, thinking about the next
poem to write

There are people eating at a table close to a large
window

The atmosphere is so relaxing in the ambiance of
the venue the everyday helter-skelter of daily life
kept at bay behind the main door to the Public
house

The pub has an atmosphere all of its own, nobody
judges one another

People are very pleasant

I feel that I have needed to relax for a very long
time for decades I have lived like a coiled spring

Ready to unwind, but have felt that it has never felt like the right time to unwind until recently

Ah my lime and soda has arrived so refreshing and relaxing

SHINE

As I gaze out of the window, I can see you bathing
in the sun's rays

The sun is warming you after being left outside in
all sorts of weather and made to stand outside
during nightfall

As I look through the window the sun is rebounding
off your surface making you shine brightly in the
light

That is until the brewery wagon takes you away to
be filled full of beer to be once more used to store
beer

A SMALL WORD

Love is such a small powerful word with such a big
meaning

Kindness is such a beautiful feeling, full of
happiness that explodes within

To have loved is a feeling that we never forget

To share a love with someone else is a bond never
to be broken

I am gearing up to let love back into my life once
again

EASTERN PROMISE

I can see a lady of grace and manners

You light up the room with your personality

You ooze with confidence you stand out from the crowd

You have left a strong impression burnt into my memory

There is something so different about you? I just cannot put my finger on what it is

There is an Eastern mystery surrounding you, which permeates my mind

FROZEN

Her face had a tint of blue, due to the coldness
outside

The coldness ran throughout her body right to the
core

Her lips had a steely blue sheen

She looked so cold, her body is in spasm, and the
coat that she was wearing was no defence against
the cold

The icicles that were dangling from her nose
seemed to grow bit by bit

Humour was not the order of the day

Lucky man Jack Frost, to get so close to her on her
final day

But alas I can only look on from afar

CLEANING DAY

Ah it feels so good, having you warm up my skin

I feel a pleasant tingle coursing through my outer skin

Oh how expectantly I wait for this day, my skin becomes alive, warming to your caress, and you can be firm but gentle

You use a cloth that you use to buff me up like a bright brass button

My timber is so shiny and smooth

Oh how I look forward to the cleaning day it is like a breath of fresh air as you buff my table top

WISHES

Follow your dreams such a powerful rallying cry

It is a strange feeling, as I was never encouraged to follow my dreams

My dreams were suppressed from an early age for many years my dreams were simmering and bubbling away beneath the surface

My dreams resurfaced many years later, it felt like a volcano that had lain dormant and suddenly erupting

It is not too late for anyone to follow their dreams in my case the volcano of the written verse suddenly spewed from within and cascaded onto the page

The time is right for everyone to be encouraged to follow their dreams

EYES

Your eyes are the biggest give away, angry eyes,
happy eyes and watch your step eyes

Eyes are the gateway to your inner self

Your laughter eyes are your most expressive
feature, when you are laughing your face beautifully
lights up. You light up and give off a warm, happy
and confident glow

I can see the girlish and impish person through your
eyes. On occasions I can see your inner self,
attractive and so you

How lucky I am to be able to see you every day the
good, bad and angry eyes

Your eyes can be so piercing and can cut the
atmosphere with just a glance

There is one thing that I do not know is the colour
of your eyes One day I will be close enough to you
to find out

I look forward to that day

WAKE UP

Do I think that I day dream well yes I do
Most of my life has been one big day dream

Who knows if my daydreams may become reality,
and what may happen if they become true

I know that life has a habit of biting a dreamer on
the bottom

Some people will say that I need to wake up to
reality

Who knows what may happen, maybe a dream may
come true

THE CARROT

I start out as a dried and shrivelled thing,
millimeters in size

When the wrapping that I am stored in is taken off, I
am plunged into a dark, wet cold substance, where I
remain motionless for weeks

I have no idea where I am, I don't know what is
happening around me

Just recently I can feel the dark substance warming

All of a sudden I seem to be growing, I am not as
shriveled anymore, I turning from a dry and
shriveled object, and I am beginning to retain
moisture

One morning I have broken away from the dark
moist substance that has entombed me for weeks

I have broken through the substance and can feel
the heat of the sun and I am in daylight

My green leaves and my orange trunk are above
ground and soaking up the daylight and the sun's
rays

The remainder of my trunk is still encased in the
dark moist soil
One summer's day I am plucked from the ground I
can hear voices they seem so excited and delighted
at what they have plucked out of the ground

A large plump straight carrot just right for the
cooking pot

PRETTY

Such a pleasant and pretty lady

I do not think that she sees herself as an attractive
person

When she lets her hair carousel down her face she
looks so much more attractive

She has such a voluptuous figure

I do not suppose she would like to be viewed in
such a way

Such a pretty lady

AT BAY

We all want happiness in our lives

For far too long I have kept my feelings at bay

Not allowing the feelings of happiness and love to
enter my life

Maybe I have become lazy and it is easier not to
become distracted by the feelings for another

THOUGHTS

Sometimes I wish for someone in my life and other times I am more than happy to be alone

I often feel that I may overpower and stifle with too much love and affection

In the end I end up pushing people away

Maybe this will be the way of things and I will remain on my own? Who knows?

I will always have my memories, which never let me down

TRAVEL

Who are the people who queue for the early
morning train, the same train that every morning
takes them to the next city

Those who travel for an hour or so, before they start
their days work

Once aboard the train they immediately open up the
screens of their laptops and immediately set to work

Others are slurping on their hot cups of coffee to
help keep them awake?

It is such a competitive world

It is a journey that I do not envy

THE MEAL

The meal before me looked very appetizing and the
aroma permeating the air smelt wonderful

It looked fit for a king, I could not wait to taste the
cornucopia of delicious food

But wait my eyes caught sight of something alien
looking on the plate

It was the dreaded mushroom I ate everything on
the plate less the mushrooms

I lined them up like little soldiers on parade

They looked unloved and unwanted and in my eyes
they were unwanted and unloved

The host looked at me in horror, I then felt the same
as the mushrooms unwanted

I can imagine what she thought of me, "how dare he, what an insult to my cooking"

I must learn to love the humble mushroom

VOICES

It is so interesting to hear so many accents and
dialects in the pub

There are well spoken and educated voices

There are the more down to earth accents

There so many dialects from around the country all
mingling in one place

There are the Northern twangs
And the Southern twangs

There is such a cacophony of sound

AUTUMN

From my window I can see for miles

I can see the sun lighting up the leaves bringing out
the colours from within the shadows

The reds, greens and yellows of the leaves against
the bright blue late autumn sky

How the autumn light changes nature from darkness
To the light and various hints of the greens, reds
and the browns

Autumn has a beauty all of its own

It will soon turn to the cold dark winter months

HATRED

We were so happy and now our feelings border on
hatred

They say that there is such a thin line between hated
and love

To think it was not so long ago
That we would talk and be so happy in one
another's company

Now we avoid one another
You cannot bear to look at me, your eyes are full of
hatred

Life is too short to be hating one another. I often
wonder what I have ever done to you

Sometimes you avoid me by running away or hide
out of view

All because you hate being in the same room as me.
What must you be thinking to hate me with so much
venom?

TEA FOR TWO

I always feel comfortable in your company
When we last met I could not keep my eyes off you

My eyes were taking in every detail on your face,
the way your mouth moved, the glint and
expression of your eyes

The smile forming on your lips
The softness of your skin, how I wanted to touch
your hand to hold it in mine

I knew it was a step too far

How we chattered and chattered I wish that we
could meet for tea for two again

98231209R10059

Made in the USA
Columbia, SC
23 June 2018